A SILENT LANGUAGE

Jon Fosse was born in 1959 on the west coast of Norway. Since his 1983 fiction debut, *Raudt, svart* [Red, Black], Fosse has written prose, poetry, essays, short stories, children's books and over forty plays. In 2023, he was awarded the Nobel Prize in Literature 'for his innovative plays and prose which give voice to the unsayable'.

Damion Searls is a translator from German, Norwegian, French and Dutch, and a writer in English. He has translated eleven books by Jon Fosse, including the three books of *Septology*.

Chris Hall is a translator from Swedish. He lives in Stockholm.

'Jon Fosse is a major European writer.'
— Karl Ove Knausgaard, author of *My Struggle*

'The Beckett of the twenty-first century.'
— *Le Monde*

'Fosse has been compared to Ibsen and to Beckett, and it is easy to see his work as Ibsen stripped down to its emotional essentials. But it is much more. For one thing, it has a fierce poetic simplicity.'
— *New York Times*

'Jon Fosse has managed, like few others, to carve out a literary form of his own.'
— Nordic Council Literature Prize

'He touches you so deeply when you read him, and when you have read one work you have to continue.... What is special with him is the closeness in his writing. It touches on the deepest feelings that you have – anxieties, insecurities, questions of life and death – such things that every human being actually confronts from the very beginning. In that sense I think he reaches very far and there is a sort of universal impact of everything that he writes. And it doesn't matter if it is drama, poetry or prose – it has the same kind of appeal to this basic humanness.'
— Anders Olsson, Nobel committee

'We are in the presence of rare literary greatness. It is for this greatness that the Swedish Academy has justly awarded Jon Fosse the Nobel Prize.'
— Paul Binding, *TLS*

'Searls is to Fosse what Anthea Bell is to W. G. Sebald, the best possible intermediary.'
— Blake Morrison, *London Review of Books*

Praise for *Septology*

'It ties *2666* by Roberto Bolaño as my favourite book from the twenty-first century.... What I read was nothing less than a desperate prayer made radiant by sudden spikes of ecstatic beauty.'
— Lauren Groff, *Literary Hub*

'Fosse has written a strange mystical moebius strip of a novel, in which an artist struggles with faith and loneliness, and watches himself, or versions of himself, fall away into the lower depths. The social world seems distant and foggy in this profound, existential narrative.'
— Hari Kunzru, author of *Red Pill*

'I hesitate to compare the experience of reading these works to the act of meditation. But that is the closest I can come to describing how something in the critical self is shed in the process of reading Fosse, only to be replaced by something more primal. A mood. An atmosphere. The sound of words moving on a page.'
— Ruth Margalit, *New York Review of Books*

'Having read the Norwegian writer Jon Fosse's *Septology*, an extraordinary seven-novel sequence about an old man's recursive reckoning with the braided realities of God, art, identity, family life and human life itself, I've come into awe and reverence myself for idiosyncratic forms of immense metaphysical fortitude.'
— Randy Boyagoda, *New York Times*

'Fosse intuitively – and with great artistry – conveys ... a sense of wonder at the unfathomable miracle of life, even in its bleakest and loneliest moments.'
— Bryan Karetnyk, *Financial Times*

'The entire septet seems to take place in a state of limbo.... Though Fosse has largely done away with punctuation altogether, opting instead for sudden line breaks, his dense, sinuous prose is never convoluted, and its effect is mesmerizing.'
— Johanna Elster Hanson, *TLS*

'The translation by Damion Searls is deserving of special recognition. His rendering of this remarkable single run-on sentence over three volumes is flawless. The rhythms, the shifts in pace, the nuances in tone are all conveyed with masterful understatement. The *Septology* series is among the highlights of my reading life.'
— Rónán Hession, *Irish Times*

'With *Septology*, Fosse has found a new approach to writing fiction, different from what he has written before and – it is strange to say, as the novel enters its fifth century – different from what has been written before. *Septology* feels new.'
— Wyatt Mason, *Harper's*

'*Septology* is the only novel I have read that has made me believe in the reality of the divine, as the fourteenth-century theologian Meister Eckhart, whom Fosse has read intently, describes it: "It is in darkness that one finds the light, so when we are in sorrow, then this light is nearest of all to us." None of the comparisons to other writers seem right. Bernhard? Too aggressive. Beckett? Too controlling. Ibsen? "He is the most destructive writer I know," Fosse claims. "I feel that there's a kind of – I don't know if it's a good English word – but a kind of reconciliation in my writing. Or, to use the Catholic or Christian word, peace."'
— Merve Emre, *New Yorker*

Praise for *A Shining*

'*A Shining* can be read in many ways: as a realistic monologue; as a fable; as a Christian-inflected allegory; as a nightmare painstakingly recounted the next morning, the horror of the experience still pulsing under the words, though somewhat mitigated by the small daily miracle of daylight. I think the great splendour of Fosse's fiction is that it so deeply rejects any singular interpretation; as one reads, the story does not sound a clear singular note, but rather becomes a chord with all the many possible interpretations ringing out at once. This refusal to succumb to the solitary, the stark, the simple, the binary – to insist that complicated things like death and God retain their immense mysteries and contradictions – seems, in this increasingly partisan world of ours, a quietly powerful moral stance.'
— Lauren Groff, *Guardian*

'Fosse's prose doesn't speak so much as witnesses, unfolds, accumulates. It flows like consciousness itself.... This is perhaps why *A Shining* feels so momentous, even at fewer than fifty pages. You never quite know where you're going. But it doesn't matter: you want to follow, to move in step with the rhythm of these words.'
— Matthew Janney, *Financial Times*

'The translation by Damion Searls perfectly judges the pitch and rhythm ... producing a natural reading beat.... *A Shining* is a neat example of Fosse's gift for portraying porous psychological states, and its publication is perfectly timed for a satisfying Samhain evening read.'
— Rónán Hession, *Irish Times*

'The physical and otherworldly hinterland of *A Shining* through which Jon Fosse is the guide is at once terrifying and deeply reassuring.'
— Catherine Taylor, *TLS*

'*A Shining* is marked by what is perhaps Fosse's defining skill: his ability to effortlessly marry the mundane and the sublime. The author is himself a practicing Catholic; he was received into the Church in 2012, and a certain spiritual seriousness is at the heart of his works' power, even while their spirit everywhere shuns the dogmatic. Expect from Fosse neither the supposedly infallible truths of the pulpit nor Scripture's resonant cadence. The experience of reading him is of a different order entirely, one more humble, and perhaps as illuminating.'
— Luke Warde, *Sunday Independent*

'In this spare tale of disorientation and longing, by the winner of this year's Nobel Prize in Literature, a man gets stranded on a back road in a forest and wanders deep into the trees.... Fosse uses fleeting allusions to a world beyond the reach of the narrator to explore some of humanity's most elusive pursuits, certainty and inviolability among them. His bracingly clear prose imbues the story's ambiguities with a profundity both revelatory and familiar.'
— *New Yorker*

Praise for *Aliss at the Fire*

'Prose doesn't have hooks, and Fosse's incantations are as unexcerptable as Philip Glass symphonies or Béla Tarr tracking shots.... On it goes, building layer upon layer of past and present, ancestors and loved ones, until you are immersed in that world and the prose conjures luminous glory flashing past like Blakean angels. Maybe it is convincing to say that Fosse is the only writer whose book has made me weep with emotion as I translated it.'
— Damion Searls, *Paris Review*

Fitzcarraldo Editions

A SILENT LANGAUGE

JON FOSSE'S NOBEL LECTURE

Translated by

DAMION SEARLS

It happened suddenly when I was in high school: my teacher asked me to read a passage aloud, and as if out of nowhere I felt terrified. It was completely overpowering – it was like I disappeared into the terror and nothing else was left of me. I stood up and ran out of the room.

I could feel the other students, and teacher, watching me wide-eyed as I ran out.

Afterwards, I tried to explain my strange behaviour by saying I'd needed to go to the bathroom. I could see from the faces of the people listening to this that they didn't believe me. They must have just thought I was being weird, and even well on my way to going crazy.

A fear of public speaking stayed with me. After a while, I managed to ask my teachers to excuse me from participating, since it made me so anxious; some of them believed me and stopped asking me to read aloud, while others seemed to think I was trying to play some kind of trick on them.

This experience taught me something important about people.

And it also taught me other things.

In fact, it probably taught me the thing that's the reason why I can sit here today and read out loud in public. Without any fear, or at least without almost any.

What had I learned?

In a way it was like my language had been taken from me, and I had to take it back, so to speak. And I couldn't do so on other people's terms – I had to do it on my own terms.

So I started writing my own things: short poems, little stories.

And I could feel that doing this made me feel safe – it made me feel the opposite of fear.

I had found something like a place inside me that was mine, mine alone, and from that place I could write things that were also mine alone.

Today, roughly fifty years later, I am still writing – and still from this mysterious place inside me. To tell the truth, I don't know much about this place except for the fact that it exists.

The Norwegian poet Olav H. Hauge once wrote a poem where he compared writing poetry with being a child playing in the forest, building little shelters of leaves and twigs, and then crawling inside these shelters, lighting a candle, and sitting there feeling safe in the dark autumn evenings.

I feel like this is a good image for how I, too, experience writing. Today just as much as fifty years ago.

I learned something else as well from that high school experience: I learned that, for me at least, there is an important difference between spoken and written language, or between spoken language and literary language.

Spoken language is often monologic: it communicates information, says that something is a certain way, or else it is a rhetorical act of expressing belief or trying to persuade the listener.

Literary language is never like that: it has no message; it conveys nothing; it is a kind of meaning without communication. It exists as its own thing.

And so obviously any good piece of literary writing is the complete opposite of any kind of preaching, whether religious, political, or anything else.

Through my fear of public speaking in school, I so to speak entered into the solitary life of the literary writer, where I've remained ever since.

I have written a lot of both fiction and plays.

And what makes a play a play, of course, is that it is written speech: dialogue, conversations (or often failed attempts at conversation), and whatever monologues there may be, all nonetheless existing in a written, created universe. All parts of something that doesn't inform or communicate but merely is, existing as its own thing.

When it comes to prose fiction, Mikhail Bakhtin was right to argue that the very form of literary expression, of narrative, is double-voiced.

To simplify slightly: it contains the voice of the person who decides on the words, the writer, and also the voice of the person in the story. These voices often blur and slip into each other in such a way that it's impossible to say about any given words of the text whose they are.

The narrative simply becomes a double-voiced piece of writing – which is also, of course, part of the created written universe and its logic.

Everything I have written is, as it were, its own fictional universe, its own world. A new world for each and every play or novel.

A good poem, too – and I have also written a great deal of poetry – has its own universe. It exists primarily in relation to itself, and then the person who reads the poem enters into this created written universe. The process is more like a kind of communion than any communication.

In fact, this is probably true of everything I've written.

In any case, I have certainly never written to express myself, as they say. Rather it was to get away from myself.

Now what can I say about the fact that I ended up as a playwright?

I wrote novels and poems, and had no desire to write for the theatre, but the time came when I did so because, as part of a publicly funded effort to get people to write more modern Norwegian plays, I was offered quite a large amount of money, for the impoverished writer I was at the time, to write the opening scene of a play. I ended up writing the whole play, my first, and it is still the most performed of all my plays: *Someone Is Going to Come.*

This first experience of writing a play was the biggest surprise I ever had in my life as a writer, because up until that point, both in fiction and in poetry, I had always tried to write what cannot be said in words in the usual way – in the usual spoken way. I had always tried to write the unsayable, which is exactly how the announcement of my winning the Nobel Prize put it.

What's most important in life cannot

be said, only written – to give a slight twist to the well-known remark by Jacques Derrida.

And so, in my fiction and poetry, I tried to put silent speech into words.

But when I wrote plays, I could use silent speech – I could use silence – in a completely different way. All I had to do was write 'pause' and the silent speech was right there. This word 'pause' is without a doubt the most important word in my plays, and the one I use the most often: 'long pause', 'short pause', or just 'pause'.

There can be so much in these pauses – or so little. The fact that something cannot be said, the fact that something refuses to be said, or the fact that something is best said by not saying anything.

But what I am quite sure speaks through these pauses the most is: silence.

Perhaps all the repetition in my fiction

functions similarly to the pauses in the plays. Or maybe this is a better way to put it: while there is silent speech in the plays, there is silent *language* in the novels, behind the written language, and if I'm writing well then I am necessarily writing this silent language too. As a simple, concrete example: in *Septology* this silent language is what says that the first Asle and the second Asle might be the same person; this silent language is what says that the whole long novel, some twelve hundred pages in Norwegian, might actually be the written expression of a single, long-drawn-out moment.

But silent speech, or a silent language, speaks mainly from the work as a whole. Whether the work is a novel or a play on the page or a play produced in the theatre, what matters aren't the parts in isolation but the whole, which has to be in every tiniest detail as well. I might go so far as to say that there is a spirit of the whole, a spirit that speaks, somehow, both from very nearby and from a very great distance.

And what do you hear, if you listen well enough?

You hear the silence.

And, as others have said before: It is only in the silence that we can hear the voice of God.

Well, maybe.

To come back to earth for a moment, I want to mention something else that writing for the theatre gave me. Writing is a solitary thing, as I said, and solitude is good but only as long as the road back to other people remains open, to quote another poem by Olav Hauge.

And what I felt the first time I saw something I'd written performed on stage was exactly the opposite of solitude: community. Creating art through collaboration, which made me feel a deep sense of security and happiness.

This experience stayed with me, and it is no doubt why I continued as a playwright, feeling not just peace of mind but a kind of joy, even from bad productions.

Theatre is really one large act of listening: the director has to listen to the script – or at least should listen to it – just as the actors listen to it and to one another, and to the director, and just as the audience then listens to the whole performance.

And for me, the act of writing is one of listening – when I write I never think it out in advance, I don't plan anything, I proceed by listening.

If there's any metaphor I would use for the act of writing, it would have to be listening.

And so, it almost necessarily follows, writing is like music. At one point when I was a teenager, I switched, so to speak, directly from playing music to writing. I stopped playing music altogether, and even stopped listening to music, and started writing, and in my writing I tried to create something I had experienced when playing music. And I did create that – and that is what I still do.

Something else that happens when I write – maybe it's a bit strange – is that there always comes a moment when I feel like the text has already been finished and written. It is out there somewhere, not inside me, and I just need to write it down before it disappears.

Sometimes I write it down without changing anything later; other times I have to as it were search for the text by rewriting, cutting, trying as carefully as

I can to bring out what already exists, what is already written somewhere.

After not wanting to write for the theatre, I ended up doing just that for more or less fifteen years. The plays I wrote were performed, and as time went on there started to be more and more productions, in many countries.

I still can't believe it.

Life is truly unbelievable.

In the same way, I can't believe that I'm sitting here having been awarded the Nobel Prize in Literature, trying to say something that more or less makes sense about what it means to write.

And that this prize was awarded, as I understand it, for both my plays and my fiction.

After many years writing plays, I suddenly felt that enough was enough – more than enough – and I decided to stop.

But writing had become a habit, one I couldn't live without – maybe, as Marguerite Duras called it, a kind of sickness – and so I decided to go back to where it had all started and write fiction, along with poems here and there, as I had for a decade or so before my first play.

And that's what I've done for the past ten or fifteen years. When I started writing fiction seriously again, I wasn't sure I could still do it. I first wrote the novel *Trilogy*, and being awarded the Nordic Council Literature Prize for it came as an important confirmation that I had something to offer as a fiction writer too.

Then I wrote *Septology*.

I experienced some of my happiest moments ever as a writer in the course of writing that novel, for example when the first Asle finds the other Asle lying in the snow and saves his life. Or at the end, when the main character, the first Asle, sets out by boat on his final journey, with his best and only friend, Åsleik, to celebrate Christmas with Åsleik's sister.

I had no intention of writing a long novel, but the novel wrote itself, so to speak, and it became a long novel, and there were many passages I wrote so smoothly and easily that everything came out right the first time.

That is probably when I am closest to what you'd call happiness.

Throughout *Septology*, there are many moments that recall or evoke things from the other books and plays I've written, but these moments are seen in a different light. And there being no full stops in the whole long novel isn't just a gimmick, something I arbitrarily made up – that's how the novel wrote itself, in a single, flowing movement that didn't need a full stop.

I said in an interview once that writing is a kind of prayer. I felt very embarrassed when I saw those words in print afterwards. But some time later, I read that Kafka had said the same thing, and I felt much better. So maybe... after all?

My early books got terrible reviews, and I decided that I simply had to stop listening to the critics. I had to trust myself and keep doing what I needed to do. If I hadn't decided that, I would have stopped writing forty years ago, after my first novel, *Red, Black*, came out.

Since then I have mostly gotten good reviews, and even prizes sometimes – but I thought it was important to follow the same logic and not let the good reviews influence me any more than the bad ones. I would stick to my own kind of writing and keep doing what I had to do.

I think I've managed to do that, and to

be honest I think I will be able to keep doing it, even after winning the Nobel Prize.

When the Prize was announced many people sent me emails and other congratulations, and of course I was glad to get them. Most of the messages were simple and happy, but some people wrote that they had screamed with joy, others that they had started crying. It was very moving.

One thing moved me more than anything else. There are a number of suicides in my novels and plays, more than I like to remember. I have sometimes worried that this justifies or legitimizes suicide, in a way. So it was especially moving when some people wrote to tell me explicitly that my writing had saved their life.

I've always known that writing can save lives, in a sense – it's probably fair to say that it has sometimes saved mine.

But nothing would make me happier than if my writing could help save other people's lives as well.

Thank you to the Swedish Academy for awarding me the Nobel Prize in Literature.

And thanks be to God.

Stockholm, 7 December 2023

Award Ceremony Speech by Professor Anders Olsson, Member of the Swedish Academy, Chair of the Nobel Committee for Literature, 10 December 2023

Your Majesties, Esteemed Nobel Prize Laureates, Ladies and Gentlemen:

To enter the world of Jon Fosse is to set foot in a domain beset by the greatest anxiety and torment of indecision. His rich oeuvre revolves around the disorientation of the individual and the difficulties experienced in finding a path in life. Whether in prose, drama or poetry, his writing approaches a state of uncertainty that can open a relation to the divine. With commonplace words here seeming inadequate, Fosse's rare quality is that he succeeds, as the award citation reads, in 'giving voice to the unsayable'.

Early on in his authorship, Fosse captures the unsayable in his short prose piece *I Couldn't Say It to You* from

1991. Here we meet an old man who is unable to rid himself of the vivid memory of something he has failed to say to his beloved throughout all their years together. He has not forgotten the look in her eyes as she sits alone at a table in the school cafeteria, a memory that remains lodged in his mind from that day forward. This is the case even on her deathbed; words and life have drifted apart. But when Fosse allows the old man to voice the unsaid, the impossible is transformed into both a touching elegy and a triumph over speechlessness.

In the late masterpiece *Septology*, completed in 2021, the main character Asle is an older artist who, in the spirit of the medieval Christian mystic Meister Eckhart, turns in prayer to a God beyond all concepts and ideas. Both in the earlier story and here in this later novel, the protagonist is nevertheless filled with an anxiety which creates a tension between the mundane and the divine. It is this anxiety that lends the work its internal drama.

Jon Fosse is not a difficult writer. He uses the simplest of words and writes about experiences to which we can all relate: separation, death and the vulnerability of love. If there is a difficulty with Fosse it concerns the reader's willingness to open herself up to the existential uncertainty he reflects on. But the fact that he is one of today's most widely performed playwrights indicates that this is a torment shared by many.

What is remarkable about Fosse's simplicity is that it gains depth and intensity through repetition and variation. In his harrowing early novel *Closed Guitar*, in which a mother locks herself out of her flat and can't get back inside to her baby, a sense of panic suffuses the language. In the shimmering world of *Morning and Evening*, anxiety turns to wonder and profound consolation as an old man named Johannes awakes one morning to find he is dying and begins to lose his sense of reality. In *Septology*, the rolling prose devoid of sentence breaks becomes one with the painter Asle's wandering thoughts, drawing the reader in with hypnotic power.

Either Fosse focuses on the unsayable, as in these works, or he chooses the language of silence, as in his radical renewal of world drama during the 1990s. Beginning with *Someone Is Going to Come*, the play with which he made his international breakthrough, he discovers how to allow speechlessness to materialize on stage. In the theatre, all that is internal must be revealed, and even what cannot be said must be given a voice. This is demonstrated in a long series of emotionally charged plays that includes *The Name*, *Dream of*

Autumn and *Death Variations*. Here, time expands to allow the dead to take their place on stage.

Jon Fosse is the first Nobel Prize laureate in Literature to write in Nynorsk and, like his great Norwegian predecessor Tarjei Vesaas, he combines strong local ties with a belief in the possibilities of contemporary literature. He shies away from what we might consider definitive wording, making it almost impossible to quote him. As such, he is the master of ambivalence and of the unresolved. In his world, uncertainty pulses with a secret light.

Dear Jon Fosse, allow me to convey the warm congratulations of the Swedish Academy, while asking you to step forward to receive, from the hand of his Majesty the King, the Nobel Prize in Literature.

Translated from Swedish by Chris Hall

The Nobel Banquet Speech

Your Majesties
Your Royal Highnesses
Excellencies
Esteemed Laureates
Ladies and Gentlemen

Many years ago, I saw myself – not in a dream, or in a daydream, more like in a vision – walking along the side of a road leading to the centre of a town.

When I saw myself there, some day in the future, I saw myself walking as someone who had received the Nobel Prize in Literature.

Because of this vision – to be honest with you, I felt rather sure that I one day would be standing here.

Thank you to the Nobel Foundation for organizing everything so well.

Thank you to the Swedish Academy for awarding me the Nobel Prize in Literature.

And thanks be to God.

Stockholm, 10 December 2023

Prose by Jon Fosse
(in chronological order)

Raudt, svart (1983)
Stengd gitar (1985)
Blod. Steinen er (1987)
Frå telling via showing til writing (1989)
Uendelig seint (1989)
Naustet (1989), translated into English as *Boathouse* by May-Brit Akerholt (Dalkey Archive, 2017). New translation forthcoming from Damion Searls.
Kant (1990)
Flaskesamlaren (1991)
Bly og vatn (1992)
Dyrehagen Hardanger (1993)
To forteljingar (1993)
Prosa frå ein oppvekst (1994)
Vått og svart (1994)
Melancholia I (1995), translated into English as *Melancholy* by Grethe Kvernes and Damion Searls (Dalkey Archive, 2006). Revised and published as *Melancholy I-II*, tr. Damion Searls and Grethe Kvernes (Fitzcarraldo Editions, 2023)
Nei å nei (1995)
Du å du (1996)
Melancholia II (1996), translated into English as *Melancholy II* by Eric Dickens (Dalkey Archive, 2014), and translated again by Damion Searls for the publication of *Melancholy I-II*, tr. Damion Searls and Grethe Kvernes (Fitzcarraldo Editions, 2023)
Fy å fy (1997)
Eldre kortare prosa med 7 bilete av Camilla Wærenskjold (1998)
Gnostiske essay (1999)
Morgon og kveld (2000), translated into English as *Morning and Evening*, tr. Damion Searls (Dalkey Archive, 2015; Fitzcarraldo Editions, 2024)

Søster (2000)
Det er Ales (2004), translated into English as *Aliss at the Fire* by Damion Searls (Dalkey Archive, 2010; revised translation for Fitzcarraldo Editions, 2023)
Andvake (2007)
Spelejenta (2009)
Kortare prosa (2011)
Olavs draumar (2012)
Kveldsvævd (2014)
Trilogien (2014), translated into English as *Trilogy* by May-Brit Akerholt (Dalkey Archive, 2016). Compiles three novellas: *Wakefulness*, *Olav's Dreams* and *Weariness*. New translation forthcoming from Damion Searls.
Levande stein (2015)
Når ein engel går gjennom scenen og andre essay (2014), translated into English as *An Angel Walks Through the Stage: and Other Essays* by May-Brit Akerholt (Dalkey Archive, 2015)
Scenes from a Childhood, translated into English by Damion Searls (Fitzcarraldo Editions, 2018). Collects texts from various sources.
Det andre namnet – Septologien I-II (2019), translated into English as *The Other Name: Septology I-II* by Damion Searls (Fitzcarraldo Editions, 2019)
Eg er ein annan – Septologien III-V (2020), translated into English as *I Is Another: Septology III-V* by Damion Searls (Fitzcarraldo Editions, 2020)
Eit nytt namn – Septologien VI-VII (2021), translated into English as *A New Name: Septology VI-VII* by Damion Searls (Fitzcarraldo Editions, 2021)
Septologien (2022), translated into English as *Septology* by Damion Searls (Fitzcarraldo Editions, 2022)
Kvitleik (2023), translated into English as *A Shining* by Damion Searls (Fitzcarraldo Editions, 2023)

Plays by Jon Fosse
(in chronological order)

Og aldri skal vi skiljast (1994)
Namnet (1995, 1998, 2008)
Nokon kjem til å kome (1996, 2004, 2018)
Barnet/Mor og barn/Sonen (1997)
Gitarmannen (1997)
Natta syng sine songar/Ein sommars dag (1998), translated into English as *Nightsongs* by Gregory Motton (Oberon, 2022)
Teaterstykke 1 (1999)
Draum om hausten (1999, 2016)
Besøk/Vinter/Ettermiddag (2000)
Teaterstykke 2 (2001)
Vakkert (2001)
Dødsvariasjonar (2002)
Jenta i sofaen (2003), translated into English as *The Girl on the Sofa* by David Harrower (Oberon, 2002)
Lilla/Suzannah (2004)
Dei døde hundane/Sa ka la (2005), translated into English as *The Dead Dogs* by May-Brit Akerholt (Oberon, 2014)
Teaterstykke 3 (2005)
Svevn/Varmt (2006)
Rambuku/Skuggar (2007)
Eg er vinden (2008), translated into English as *I Am the Wind* by Simon Stephens (Oberon, 2011)
Desse auga (2009)
Teaterstykke 4 (2009)
Jente i gul regnjakke (2010)
Kortare stykke (2011)
Hav (2014)
Tre librettoar (2015)
Teaterstykke 5 (2016)
Fem teaterstykke (2019)
Slik var det (2020)
Sterk vind. Eit scenisk dikt (2021)
I svarte skogen inne (2023)
Einkvan (2024)

Poetry by Jon Fosse
(in chronological order)

Engel med vatn i augene (1986)
Hundens bevegelsar (1990)
Hund og engel (1992)
Dikt 1986–1992 (1995)
Nye dikt 1991–1994 (1997)
Dikt 1986–2001 (2001)
Auge i vind (2003)
Dikt i samling (2009)
Songar (2009)
Stein til stein (2013)
Poesiar (2016)
Ro mitt Hav (2019)
Dikt i samling (2021)

This book is printed with plant-based inks on materials certified by the Forest Stewardship Council®. The FSC® promotes an ecologically, socially and economically responsible management of the world's forests. This book has been printed without the use of plastic-based coatings.

Fitzcarraldo Editions
8-12 Creekside
London, SE8 3DX
United Kingdom

Originally published in Great Britain
by Fitzcarraldo Editions in 2024

ISBN 978-1-80427-123-0

Design by Ray O'Meara
Typeset in Fitzcarraldo
Printed and bound by TJ Books Limited

fitzcarraldoeditions.com

Fitzcarraldo Editions